ICE-CREAMS

This book was created in 2012 for Lakeland by AWW Books, an imprint of Octopus Publishing Group Ltd, based on materials licensed to it by ACP Magazines Ltd, a division of PBL Media Pty Limited.

54 Park St, Sydney
GPO Box 4088, Sydney, NSW 2001
phone (02) 9282 8618; fax (02) 9267 9438
acpbooks@acpmagazines.com.au;
www.acpbooks.com.au

OCTOPUS PUBLISHING GROUP
Design – Chris Bell
Food Director – Pamela Clark

Published for Lakeland in the United Kingdom by Octopus Publishing Group Limited

Endeavour House
189 Shaftesbury Avenue
London WC2H 8JY
United Kingdom
phone + 44 (0) 207 632 5400;
fax + 44 (0) 207 632 5405
aww@octopusbooks.co.uk;
www.octopusbooks.co.uk
www.australian-womens-weekly.com

Printed and bound in China

A catalogue record for this book is available from the British Library.

ISBN 978-1-907428-72-2

The Department of Health advises that eggs should not be consumed raw. This book contains some dishes made with raw or lightly cooked eggs. It is prudent for vulnerable people such as pregnant and nursing mothers, invalids, the elderly, babies and young children to avoid uncooked or lightly cooked dishes made with eggs. Once prepared, these dishes should be kept refrigerated and used promptly.

This book also includes dishes made with nuts and nut derivatives. It is advisable for those with known allergic reactions to nuts and nut derivatives and those who may be potentially vulnerable to these allergies, such as pregnant and nursing mothers, invalids, the elderly, babies and children to avoid dishes made with nuts and nut oils. It is also prudent to check the labels of pre-prepared ingredients for the possible inclusion of nut derivatives.

Some of the recipes in this book have appeared in other publications.

ICE-CREAMS

Nothing beats homemade ice-cream, be it a fruit lolly to refresh on a summer day or a lavish creamy concoction to impress at a dinner party. This collection of over 60 recipes offers an array of icy treats from White Christmas Ice-cream and Banana Caramel Sundae to Raspberry Sorbet and Mango Frozen Yogurt.

One of an exciting new series of cookbooks from Lakeland, *Ice-creams* is packed with delicious colour photos and expert hints, tips and techniques for beginners and experienced cooks alike.

With every recipe triple-tested® for perfect results, these excellent cookbooks are sure to be some of the best-loved on your kitchen bookshelf. To discover the rest of the range, together with our unrivalled selection of creative kitchenware, visit one of our friendly Lakeland stores or shop online at www.lakeland.co.uk.

CONTENTS

THE BASICS

Everyone loves ice-cream and, once you've made your own, there will be no going back to shop-bought! Here are a few hints and tips to get you started.

ICE-CREAM MAKERS

Although all the recipes in this book can be made without an ice-cream maker, if you like homemade ice-cream, an ice-cream maker is a worthwhile investment. It takes all the labour out of making ice-cream and the results are lighter, creamier and more velvety than making ice-cream or sorbet by hand.

There are two types of ice-cream makers:

Ice-cream maker with a detachable bowl This has a detachable double-walled bowl which contains a freezing agent between the two walls. You place the bowl in the freezer for 12–24 hours before you want to make ice-cream (the amount of time will depend on the model you have). Once frozen, the bowl is put into your ice-cream machine and the machine is switched on. You then add your ice-cream mixture and the paddles rotate, stirring the mixture as it gradually freezes. An average of 20–30 minutes later, your ice-cream is ready.

The advantage of this type of ice-cream maker is that it is relatively inexpensive. The downsides are that you have to plan well ahead and can't whip up a batch of ice-cream at the last minute. Also, you can only make one batch at a time as the bowl needs to be frozen again. For some models of ice-cream maker, you can buy extra bowls which solves this problem, but can take up a lot of freezer space.

Fully automatic ice-cream maker
The second kind of ice-cream maker has a freezing mechanism built in so doesn't need a pre-chilled bowl, which means you can make ice-cream whenever the fancy takes you. The machine is switched on and within a few minutes, as soon as the correct temperature is reached, the ice-cream mixture can be poured in, the paddle switched on and your ice-cream is ready in about 20–40 minutes. Several batches of ice-cream, perhaps of different flavours, can be made without delay which is handy if you want to make lots of ice-cream.

The disadvantages of these machines are that they are more expensive and quite bulky. Another point to consider is that generally they cannot be moved without waiting 12 hours before use as moving interferes with the cooling mechanism in the machine. So they ideally need to be kept permanently positioned for use which can take up a fair bit of kitchen counter space.

A WORD ABOUT INGREDIENTS

The quality of your ingredients will be reflected in the taste of your ice-cream or sorbet so it is really worth using the best and freshest you can. Eggs, milk and cream should be as fresh as possible and free-range or organic, if possible.

Because, unlike commercially made ice-cream, you will be using all natural ingredients, ice-creams and sorbets can freeze very solid so you will need to let them soften in the refrigerator about 15–30 minutes before you want to serve. You will also find that mixtures that contain alcohol or a high proportion of sugar will usually take longer to freeze.

KNOW YOUR ICES

- **Ice-cream** is usually made of a custard base consisting of milk, cream, sugar and eggs. It is churned, either manually or in an ice-cream maker, which gives is a smooth, light texture.
- **Gelato** is the Italian word for ice-cream. It is made with milk, cream, sugar and various flavourings, such as fresh fruit, chocolate and nut purées. Traditional gelato differs from ice-cream in that it is made with a greater proportion of milk to cream than ice-cream so it is lower in fat and is usually served at a slightly warmer temperature, rather than completely frozen.
- **Semifreddo** As the name suggests (it is Italian for 'half-frozen'), this dessert is not quite ice-cream. It has the velvety texture of frozen mousse and melts in the mouth quicker than ice-cream.
- **Parfait**, meaning 'perfect' in French, is a frozen dessert made with eggs, cream, sugar and various flavourings such as fruit, nuts and chocolate. Soft cheeses like ricotta and mascarpone can also be used in parfaits.
- **Sorbet** is made from puréed fruit or fruit juice, a sugar syrup and sometimes egg white. It is churned in the same way as ice-cream which gives it a smooth, soft, snowy texture. It is served as a dessert and sometimes as a palate cleanser between courses.
- **Granita**, made in the same way as sorbet, has larger, coarse, shard-like ice crystals. It is ideally suited to making by hand – which is done by dragging a fork across the frozen surface of the granita to produce big ice crystals – but can also be partially made in an ice-cream maker to speed up the process.

THE IMPORTANCE OF KITCHEN HYGIENE

Ice-cream is a dairy product so hygiene and basic food safety are especially important.

- Homemade ice-cream can be stored in the freezer for up to 2 weeks.
- It is wise to leave ice-cream in the fridge rather than at room temperature to soften slightly before serving to avoid exposing it to food-poisoning bacteria such as staphylococci. Return the ice-cream to the freezer as soon as you've finished serving.
- Never re-freeze ice-cream that has melted.
- Always wash your hands before beginning to prepare a recipe and after handling eggs.
- Ice-creams can contain raw or partially cooked eggs so should be avoided by anyone who might be particularly vulnerable to salmonella, such as pregnant women, the elderly, babies and toddlers.
- Once prepared ice-creams and frozen desserts should be frozen promptly.
- Store ice-cream in a container with a tightly sealed lid.
- Keep all utensils and your ice-cream maker scrupulously clean.

ICE-CREAMS

VANILLA ICE-CREAM

2 vanilla pods
410ml milk
580ml double cream
8 egg yolks
165g caster sugar

1 Split vanilla pods lengthways; scrape out seeds into medium saucepan. Add pods, milk and cream; bring to the boil.
2 Meanwhile, whisk egg yolks and sugar in medium bowl until creamy; gradually whisk into hot milk mixture. Stir over low heat, without boiling, until mixture thickens slightly.
3 Strain mixture into medium heatproof bowl; discard vanilla pods. Cover surface of custard with cling film; refrigerate about 1 hour or until cold.
4 Pour custard into ice-cream maker, churn according to manufacturer's instructions. (Or place custard in shallow container, such as an aluminium baking tin, cover with foil; freeze until almost firm. Place ice-cream in large bowl, chop coarsely then beat with electric mixer until smooth. Pour into deep container, cover; freeze until firm. Repeat process two more times.)

prep + cook time 25 minutes + chilling, churning & freezing time
makes about 1 litre (serves 8)

CHOCOLATE ICE-CREAM

Omit vanilla pods; add 20g coarsely chopped dark eating chocolate to milk and cream when heating.

QUICK MANGO ICE-CREAM

500ml mango purée
125ml double cream
375ml ready-made custard
60ml lemon juice
80g icing sugar

1 Combine ingredients in large bowl.
2 Pour into ice-cream maker and churn according to manufacturer's directions. (Or, pour mixture into a loaf tin, cover with foil and freeze until a 2cm rim has formed around the edge. Transfer mixture to chilled bowl; beat with electric mixer until all ice particles have broken up. Return to tin; freeze until almost firm. Chop and beat once more. Pour mixture into loaf tin, cover with foil and freeze until firm.)

prep time 10 minutes + churning & freezing time
serves 8
tip You will need three medium (1.3kg) mangoes for this recipe.

WHITE CHRISTMAS ICE-CREAM

1 vanilla pod
430ml milk
580ml double cream
180g white eating chocolate, chopped coarsely
8 egg yolks
165g caster sugar
130g dried cranberries
2 tablespoons brandy
140g unsalted pistachios
2 teaspoons vegetable oil

1 Split vanilla pod lengthways; scrape seeds into medium saucepan. Add pod, milk, cream and 50g of the chocolate; bring to the boil.
2 Meanwhile, whisk egg yolks and sugar in medium bowl until thick and creamy; gradually whisk into hot milk mixture. Stir custard over low heat, without boiling, until thickened slightly. Strain into medium heatproof bowl. Cover surface of custard with cling film; refrigerate about 1 hour or until cold.
3 Pour custard into ice-cream maker, churn according to manufacturer's instructions. (Or place custard in shallow container, such as an aluminium baking tin, cover with foil; freeze until almost firm. Place ice-cream in large bowl, chop coarsely then beat with electric beater until smooth. Pour into deep container, cover; freeze until firm. Repeat process two more times.)
4 Meanwhile, place cranberries and brandy in small bowl; stand 15 minutes.
5 Stir cranberry mixture and nuts into ice-cream. Spoon ice-cream into eight 180ml moulds. Cover; freeze 3 hours or until firm.
6 Stir remaining chocolate and oil in small saucepan over low heat until smooth.
7 Dip each mould, one at a time, into a bowl of hot water for about 1 second. Turn ice-creams onto serving plates; top with warm chocolate mixture.

prep + cook time 1 hour + chilling, churning & freezing time
serves 8

DARK CHOCOLATE & ORANGE ICE-CREAM

430ml milk
580ml double cream
1 tablespoon cocoa powder
100g dark eating chocolate, chopped coarsely
8 egg yolks
165g caster sugar
2 tablespoons orange-flavoured liqueur

for chocolate orange bombes
6 whole glacé clementines
300g dark eating chocolate, chopped coarsely
2 teaspoons vegetable oil
2 teaspoons cocoa powder

1 Combine milk, cream, sifted cocoa and chocolate in medium saucepan; bring to the boil, stirring.
2 Meanwhile, whisk egg yolks and sugar in medium bowl until thick and creamy; gradually whisk into hot milk mixture. Stir custard over low heat, without boiling, until thickened slightly. Stir in liqueur. Strain into medium heatproof bowl. Cover surface of custard with cling film; refrigerate about 1 hour or until cold.
3 Pour custard into ice-cream maker, churn according to manufacturer's instructions. (Or place custard in shallow container, such as an aluminium baking tin, cover with foil; freeze until almost firm. Place ice-cream in large bowl, chop coarsely then beat with electric beater until smooth. Pour into deep container, cover; freeze until firm. Repeat process two more times.)

for chocolate orange bombes
Line six 250ml moulds with cling film. Stand ice-cream at room temperature to soften slightly; spoon half of the ice-cream into the moulds. Using the back of a teaspoon, make a shallow hollow in the centre of ice-cream. Place one clementine in each hollow; top with remaining ice-cream. Smooth surface; cover, freeze 3 hours or until firm. Turn puddings onto a tray; return to freezer. Cut six 14cm rounds from cling film or resealable plastic bags. Stir remaining chocolate and oil in small saucepan over low heat until smooth. Spread melted chocolate over cling film then quickly drape film, chocolate-side down, over puddings. Quickly smooth with hands, to avoid making deep pleats in the film. Freeze until firm; peel away film. Serve bombes dusted with sifted cocoa.

prep + cook time 1 hour + chilling, churning & freezing time
serves 6
tip You can use Cointreau or any other orange-flavoured liqueur.

BURNT BROWN SUGAR ICE-CREAM WITH PISTACHIO PRALINE

165g light brown sugar
60ml orange juice
430ml milk
580ml double cream
8 egg yolks

pistachio praline
165g caster sugar
80ml water
45g pistachios, roasted

1 Stir sugar and juice in medium saucepan over heat, without boiling, until sugar dissolves. Bring to the boil; reduce heat, simmer, uncovered, without stirring, about 7 minutes or until mixture is dark brown in colour. Remove from heat, gradually stir in combined milk and cream; stir over heat until toffee dissolves and mixture is smooth.
2 Using electric mixer, beat egg yolks in medium bowl until thick and creamy; gradually beat in hot milk mixture. Pour custard mixture into large pan; stir over low heat, without boiling, until mixture thickens slightly and coats the back of a wooden spoon. Immediately strain custard mixture into a medium heatproof bowl. Cover surface with cling film; refrigerate 1 hour or until cold.
3 Pour custard into ice-cream maker, churn according to manufacturer's instructions. Pour into 2 litre pudding basin as soon as churning process is completed. (Or place custard in shallow container, such as an aluminium baking tin, cover with foil; freeze until almost firm. Place ice-cream in large bowl, chop coarsely then beat with electric beater until smooth. Pour into deep container, cover; freeze until firm. Repeat process two more times. Pour into 2 litre pudding basin after last beating. Freeze until firm.)
4 Meanwhile, make pistachio praline.
5 Dip pudding bowl into hot water for 10 seconds; turn ice-cream onto plate. Press pistachio praline all over ice-cream to coat; freeze 1 hour before serving.

pistachio praline Stir sugar and the water in small saucepan over heat, without boiling, until sugar dissolves. Bring to the boil; boil 5 minutes or until golden caramel in colour. Place nuts on oiled oven tray; pour toffee over nuts, stand until set. Break praline into small pieces; process until chopped finely.

prep + cook time 50 minutes + chilling, churning & freezing time
serves 8
tips Ice-cream can be made up to three days ahead. Praline can be pressed onto ice-cream up to a day in advance. Cover tightly with cling film and freeze until required.

ALMOND MILK ICE-CREAM WITH POACHED PLUMS

500ml water
70g toasted slivered almonds
1 vanilla pod
300ml double cream
165g caster sugar
6 egg yolks

poached plums
500ml water
250ml port
110g caster sugar
1 cinnamon stick
4 plums (450g), halved, stones removed

1 Blend or process the water and nuts until fine. Strain almond milk through a muslin-lined strainer into medium saucepan; discard solids.
2 Halve vanilla pod lengthways, scrape seeds into pan with almond milk. Add pod with cream and 60g of the sugar to pan; bring to a boil. Remove from heat; stand 30 minutes. Discard pod.
3 Beat egg yolks and remaining sugar in medium bowl with electric mixer until thick and creamy. Gradually stir in almond mixture; return to same pan. Cook, stirring, over low heat, without boiling until mixture thickens slightly. Remove from heat. Pour into medium heatproof bowl. Cover surface of custard with cling film; refrigerate about 1 hour or until cold.
4 Pour custard into ice-cream maker, churn according to manufacturer's instructions. (Or line 14cm x 21cm loaf tin with baking parchment. Pour custard into loaf tin, cover with foil, freeze until firm. Remove ice-cream from freezer, turn into large bowl; chop ice-cream coarsely then beat with electric beater until smooth. Return to loaf tin, cover. Freeze until firm.)
5 Serve ice-cream topped with plums and syrup.

poached plums Stir the water, port, sugar and cinnamon in medium saucepan, without boiling, until sugar dissolves. Add plums; cook, uncovered, over low heat, about 30 minutes or until just tender. Remove plums from syrup; discard skins. Bring syrup to a boil; boil, uncovered, about 10 minutes or until syrup is reduced to about 250ml. Remove from heat, discard cinnamon; cool 10 minutes. Refrigerate, covered, until cold.

prep + cook time 1 hour + chilling, churning & freezing time
serves 8

CASSATA

2 eggs, separated
80g icing sugar
125ml double cream
few drops almond essence

second layer
2 eggs, separated
80g icing sugar
125ml double cream
60g dark eating chocolate, melted
2 tablespoons cocoa powder
1½ tablespoons water

third layer
250ml double cream
1 teaspoon vanilla extract
1 egg white, beaten lightly
55g icing sugar
2 tablespoons red glacé cherries, chopped finely
2 glacé apricots, chopped finely
2 glacé pineapple rings, chopped finely
1 tablespoon green glacé cherries, chopped finely
30g flaked almonds, toasted

1 Beat egg whites in small bowl with electric mixer until firm peaks form; gradually beat in sifted icing sugar. Fold in lightly beaten egg yolks.
2 Beat cream and almond essence in small bowl with electric mixer until soft peaks form; fold into egg mixture. Pour mixture into deep 20cm-round cake tin. Level top; freeze until firm.
3 Make second layer and spread over almond layer; freeze until firm.
4 Make third layer and spread over second layer; freeze until firm.
5 Run small spatula around edge of cassata; wipe hot cloth over base and side of tin. Turn cassata onto serving plate.

second layer Beat egg whites in small bowl with electric mixer until firm peaks form; gradually beat in sifted icing sugar. Beat cream in small bowl until soft peaks form; fold into egg white mixture. Place chocolate in small bowl; stir in egg yolks. Stir blended cocoa and water into chocolate mixture; fold chocolate mixture through cream mixture.

third layer Beat cream and extract in small bowl with electric mixer until firm peaks form. Beat egg white in small bowl with electric mixer until soft peaks form; gradually add sifted icing sugar. Fold egg white mixture into cream; fold in fruit and nuts.

prep + cook time about 1 hour + freezing time
serves 8
tip Cassata can be made a week ahead; keep, covered, in freezer.

HONEY BUTTERMILK ICE-CREAM

60ml water
2 teaspoons powdered gelatine
375ml low-fat evaporated milk
175g honey
375ml buttermilk

1 Place the water in small heatproof jug; sprinkle over gelatine. Stand jug in small saucepan of simmering water, stirring, until gelatine dissolves.
2 Meanwhile, place evaporated milk in medium saucepan; bring to the boil. Remove from heat; stir in honey and gelatine mixture. Transfer mixture to medium bowl; cool to room temperature.
3 Beat buttermilk in small bowl with electric mixer until frothy; transfer to large jug. Beat evaporated milk mixture in large bowl with electric mixer until light and frothy. Gradually beat in buttermilk until combined.
4 Pour custard into ice-cream maker, churn according to manufacturer's instructions. (Or pour mixture into 2-litre metal container. Cover tightly with foil, freeze 3 hours or overnight. Beat ice-cream in large bowl with electric mixer until smooth. Return to container, cover; freeze for further 3 hours or until firm.)
5 Serve ice-cream with fresh fruit, if desired.

prep + cook time 50 minutes + cooling, churning & freezing time
serves 8

CHOCOLATE HAZELNUT GELATO

125g hazelnuts
400ml milk
600ml double cream
6 egg yolks
75g caster sugar
215g chocolate hazelnut spread

1 Preheat oven to 180°C/160°C fan-assisted. Roast hazelnuts in shallow baking dish about 8 minutes or until skins begin to split. Place nuts in clean tea towel and rub vigorously to remove skins. Chop nuts coarsely. Place nuts in medium saucepan with milk and cream; bring to a boil. Cover, remove from heat.
2 Whisk egg yolks and sugar in medium bowl until creamy; gradually whisk hot milk mixture into egg mixture. Return to pan, stir over low heat, without boiling, until mixture thickens slightly and coats the back of a spoon. Whisk in chocolate hazelnut spread.
3 Transfer mixture to large jug or bowl, cover surface with cling film; refrigerate 2 hours.
4 Strain mixture into jug to remove nuts. Pour mixture into ice-cream maker; churn according to manufacturer's instructions. (Or place custard in shallow container, such as aluminium cake tin, cover with foil, freeze until almost firm. Place mixture in large bowl, chop coarsely then beat with electric mixer until smooth. Pour into deep container, cover; for 3 hours or until firm. Repeat process two more times.)

prep + cook time 40 minutes + chilling, churning & freezing time
serves 8

GREEN TEA ICE-CREAM

2 tablespoons green tea powder
2 tablespoons boiling water
1 tablespoon caster sugar
1 vanilla pod
250ml milk
2 egg yolks
55g caster sugar, extra
300ml double cream, whipped

1 Combine tea, the water and sugar in small bowl; stand 10 minutes.
2 Split vanilla pod lengthways; scrape out seeds. Combine pod, seeds and milk in small saucepan; bring to a boil. Stir in tea mixture; stand 5 minutes.
3 Meanwhile, whisk egg yolks and extra sugar in small bowl until creamy; gradually whisk into hot milk mixture. Stir over low heat, without boiling, until mixture thickens slightly.
4 Strain mixture into medium heatproof bowl; discard pod. Cover surface of custard with cling film; cool. Refrigerate about 1 hour or until cold.
5 Fold whipped cream into cold custard. Pour mixture into ice-cream maker; churn according to manufacturer's instructions. (Or place custard in shallow container, cover with foil; freeze until almost firm. Place ice-cream in large bowl, chop coarsely then beat with electric mixer until smooth. Cover; freeze until firm. Repeat process twice more.)
6 Serve with fresh fruit, if desired.

prep + cook time 25 minutes + chilling, churning & freezing time
serves 4

RHUBARB CRUMBLE ICE-CREAM

220g chopped rhubarb
2 tablespoons brown sugar
2 litres vanilla ice-cream (see page 12), softened slightly
125g ginger nut biscuits, chopped coarsely

1 Line 14cm x 21cm loaf tin with cling film.
2 Cook rhubarb and sugar in large heavy-based saucepan, covered, about 5 minutes or until rhubarb is almost tender. Reduce heat; simmer, uncovered, about 5 minutes or until rhubarb softens but retains shape. Cool.
3 Place ice-cream in large bowl; break up slightly. Gently swirl in biscuits and rhubarb mixture.
4 Pour ice-cream mixture into prepared tin. Cover; freeze 3 hours or until firm.

prep + cook time 20 minutes + cooling & freezing time
serves 8

CHOCOLATE HONEYCOMB ICE-CREAM WITH CHOCOLATE CRUNCH SHARDS

500ml milk
300ml double cream
5 egg yolks
110g caster sugar
1 tablespoon custard powder
100g dark eating chocolate, chopped finely
60ml coffee-flavoured liqueur
40g chocolate honeycomb bars, chopped coarsely

chocolate crunch shards
200g dark chocolate, melted
10g chocolate honeycomb bars, chopped finely

1 Grease six 180ml dishes; line with cling film, bringing film 5cm over sides. Freeze until ready to use.
2 Combine milk and cream in medium saucepan, bring to the boil. Whisk egg yolks, sugar and custard powder in medium bowl until combined, gradually whisk in hot milk mixture. Add chocolate, stir until melted; stir in liqueur. Pour into medium heatproof bowl. Cover surface of custard with cling film; refrigerate about 1 hour or until cold.
3 Pour custard into ice-cream maker and churn according to manufacturer's instructions. Add chocolate honeycomb in last 2–3 minutes of churning. (Or pour mixture into 20cm x 30cm baking tin, cover, freeze until ice-cream is almost set. Chop ice-cream roughly, beat in large bowl with electric beater, or process, until smooth. Stir chocolate honeycomb into ice-cream.)
4 Spoon ice-cream into prepared dishes, smooth top, tap gently on counter to remove air bubbles. Enclose dishes in cling film, freeze until firm.
5 To serve, turn ice-cream onto plates, remove film, gently press chocolate shards around sides. Serve immediately.

chocolate crunch shards Spread melted chocolate evenly over 2 sheets of baking parchment, each about 26cm x 28cm; sprinkle finely chopped honeycomb evenly over chocolate, leave to set. Carefully remove chocolate from paper, break into long shards, measuring about 3cm x 13cm.

prep + cook time 45 minutes + chilling, churning & freezing time
serves 6

LOW-FAT VANILLA ICE-CREAM WITH MANGO COULIS

30g custard powder
750ml low-fat milk
110g caster sugar
300g soft tofu
2 teaspoons vanilla extract

mango coulis
1 medium mango (430g), chopped
2 tablespoons water

1 Blend custard powder with a little of the milk in medium saucepan until smooth. Add remaining milk and sugar; cook, stirring, over heat until custard boils and thickens. Remove from heat.
2 Blend or process tofu until smooth. Add tofu and extract to custard; stir to combine. Cool to room temperature.
3 Pour mixture into ice-cream maker; churn according to manufacturer's instructions. (Or transfer mixture to 14cm x 21cm loaf tin. Cover tightly with foil, freeze 3 hours or overnight. Beat ice-cream in large bowl with electric mixer until smooth. Return to loaf tin, cover; freeze for further 3 hours or until firm. Repeat beating and freezing twice more.)
4 Serve ice-cream with mango coulis.

mango coulis Blend or process mango and the water until smooth.

prep + cook time 40 minutes + chilling, churning & freezing time
serves 6
tip Ice-cream and coulis can be made 3 days ahead.

PARFAITS & FROZEN YOGURTS

RASPBERRY NOUGAT FROZEN PARFAIT

400g ricotta
165g caster sugar
300ml double cream
40g whole almonds, toasted, chopped
150g nougat, chopped
135g frozen raspberries

raspberry compote
330g frozen raspberries
55g caster sugar
500g fresh raspberries

1 Line 14cm x 21cm loaf tin with a strip of foil or baking parchment to cover the base and extend 5cm over two long sides.
2 Blend or process ricotta and sugar until smooth. Beat cream in small bowl with electric mixer until soft peaks form. Combine ricotta mixture, nuts and nougat in large bowl; fold in cream, then raspberries.
3 Spoon mixture into tin, cover with foil; freeze until firm.
4 Slice parfait, then refrigerate about 30 minutes before serving, to soften slightly.
5 Meanwhile, make berry compote.

raspberry compote Combine frozen raspberries and sugar in medium saucepan; cook, stirring, over low heat, until berries are very soft. Push raspberry mixture through coarse sieve into medium bowl; discard seeds. Just before serving, combine raspberry purée and fresh berries in medium bowl. Serve frozen parfait with raspberry compote.

prep + cook time 25 minutes + freezing & chilling time
serves 8
tips You can serve fresh berries instead of the raspberry compote, if preferred. The raspberry compote can be prepared a day ahead; keep, covered, in the refrigerator. The parfait can be made a week ahead up to step 3; slice with a knife that has been dipped in hot water, before allowing to soften in the refrigerator (step 4).

FROZEN MOCHA MOUSSE

100g dark eating chocolate, melted
2 teaspoons coffee-flavoured liqueur
2 eggs, separated
125ml double cream

milk chocolate layer
100g milk eating chocolate, melted
2 tablespoons coffee-flavoured liqueur
2 eggs, separated
125ml double cream

white chocolate layer
120g white eating chocolate, melted
60g butter, melted
2 teaspoons coffee-flavoured liqueur
3 eggs, separated
160ml double cream

nutty chocolate sauce
165g chocolate hazelnut spread
180ml double cream
1 tablespoon coffee-flavoured liqueur

1 Line 14cm x 21cm loaf tin with cling film.
2 Combine chocolate, liqueur and egg yolks in large bowl, stir until smooth. Whip cream in small bowl until soft peaks form, fold into chocolate mixture. Beat egg whites in small bowl until soft peaks form, fold into chocolate mixture.
3 Pour dark chocolate mixture into loaf tin; cover with foil, freeze until firm.
4 Make milk chocolate layer; pour over dark chocolate layer. Cover; freeze until firm.
5 Make white chocolate layer; pour over milk chocolate layer. Cover; freeze until firm.
6 Make nutty chocolate sauce.
7 Turn mousse onto serving plate; remove cling film. Slice mousse, serve with sauce.

milk chocolate layer Stir chocolate, liqueur and egg yolks in large bowl until smooth. Whip cream in small bowl until soft peaks form; fold into chocolate mixture. Beat egg whites in small bowl until soft peaks form; fold into chocolate mixture.

white chocolate layer Stir chocolate, butter, liqueur and egg yolks in large bowl until smooth. Whip cream in small bowl until soft peaks form; fold into chocolate mixture. Beat egg whites in small bowl until soft peaks form; fold into chocolate mixture.

nutty chocolate sauce Stir spread in small heatproof bowl over hot water until pourable; gradually stir in cream and liqueur. Refrigerate until cool.

prep + cook time 1 hour + freezing & chilling time
serves 10

WHITE CHOCOLATE & PISTACHIO PARFAIT

180ml double cream
250g white eating chocolate, chopped coarsely
6 egg yolks
2 eggs
110g caster sugar
400ml double cream, extra
125ml Irish cream liqueur
150g toasted shelled pistachios, chopped finely

berry compote
300g frozen mixed berries
2 tablespoons caster sugar
1 tablespoon water

1 Combine cream and chocolate in medium saucepan; stir over low heat until smooth. Beat yolks, whole eggs and sugar in small bowl with electric mixer until thick and creamy; with motor operating, gradually beat hot chocolate mixture into egg mixture. Transfer parfait mixture to large bowl, cover; refrigerate 30 minutes or until mixture thickens slightly.
2 Meanwhile, cut eight 30cm squares of baking parchment; fold one square in half diagonally. Place triangle on work top with centre point towards you; curl one point towards you, turning it under where it meets the centre point. Hold these two points together with one hand then roll remaining point towards you to meet the other two, turning it under to form a cone. Staple or tape the cone securely to hold its shape; stand cone upright in tall glass. Repeat with remaining paper squares, standing each in a tall glass; place glasses on tray.
3 Beat extra cream in small bowl with electric mixer until soft peaks form; fold into parfait mixture with liqueur and nuts. Divide mixture among cones. Cover cones loosely with cling film; freeze overnight.
4 Make berry compote.
5 Place parfaits on individual serving plates; carefully remove and discard paper. Serve with berry compote.

berry compote Combine ingredients in small saucepan; stir over low heat until sugar dissolves. Cool 10 minutes.

prep + cook time 40 minutes + chilling & freezing time
serves 8

NOUGAT SEMIFREDDO WITH ORANGE HONEY SYRUP

1 vanilla pod
3 eggs, separated
75g caster sugar
375ml double cream
200g nougat, chopped finely
75g coarsely chopped roasted shelled pistachios
1 tablespoon honey

orange honey syrup
90g honey
1 tablespoon finely grated orange rind
2 tablespoons orange juice

1 Split vanilla pod in half lengthways; scrape seeds into small bowl. Add yolks and sugar; beat with electric mixer until thick and creamy. Transfer mixture to large bowl.
2 Beat cream in small bowl with electric mixer until soft peaks form; gently fold cream into yolk mixture.
3 Beat egg whites in separate small bowl with electric mixer until soft peaks form. Gently fold half the egg whites into cream mixture; fold in nougat, nuts, honey and remaining egg white. Pour mixture into 14cm x 21cm loaf tin, cover with foil; freeze 3 hours or until just firm.
4 Make orange honey syrup.
5 Stand semifreddo at room temperature 10 minutes before serving with syrup.

orange honey syrup Bring ingredients to the boil in small saucepan. Reduce heat; simmer, uncovered, 2 minutes.

prep + cook time 25 minutes + freezing time
serves 4

ICED COCONUT SLICE

- 4 egg yolks
- 2 tablespoons caster sugar
- 100g white eating chocolate, melted
- 80ml coconut-flavoured liqueur
- 2 egg whites
- 300ml double cream, whipped
- 1 small pineapple (900g), peeled, cored, chopped finely
- 6 tablespoons finely shredded fresh mint
- 125ml pineapple juice

1 Line 14cm x 21cm loaf tin with strips of foil, extending foil 10cm over sides of tin.
2 Beat egg yolks and sugar in small bowl with electric mixer until thick and creamy; transfer mixture to large bowl. Stir in chocolate and liqueur.
3 Beat egg whites in small bowl with electric mixer until soft peaks form. Fold egg whites and cream into chocolate mixture, in two batches.
4 Pour mixture into tin; cover with foil, freeze overnight until firm.
5 Combine remaining ingredients in small bowl.
6 Serve in slices topped with pineapple mixture.

prep time 25 minutes + freezing time
serves 10

MANGO FROZEN YOGURT

- 3 egg yolks
- 150g caster sugar
- 300ml double cream
- 310ml milk
- 500g greek-style yogurt
- 2 small ripe mangoes (600g), peeled, chopped coarsely

1 Whisk egg yolks and sugar in medium bowl until light and fluffy.
2 Bring cream and milk almost to the boil in medium saucepan. Remove from heat. Whisking constantly, gradually pour cream mixture into egg mixture.
3 Return custard mixture to pan; cook over low heat, stirring constantly, until mixture thickens and coats the back of a spoon. Do not boil.
4 Transfer mixture to large bowl; cover, refrigerate until cold.
5 Stir yogurt into cold custard. Churn mixture in an ice-cream maker, following manufacturer's instructions, until beginning to thicken. Add mangoes, churn until firm. (Or freeze mixture until partially frozen; chop coarsely then beat with an electric mixer until smooth. Fold in chopped mango; freeze until firm.)
6 Transfer mixture to 1.5-litre freezer-proof container. Cover; freeze about 4 hours or until firm.
7 Serve scooped in glasses with extra sliced mango, if desired.

prep + cook time 35 minutes + chilling, churning & freezing time
serves 6
tip Store frozen yogurt, covered, in freezer for up to three months.

GREEN APPLE FROZEN YOGURT

115g honey
125ml apple juice
1 teaspoon gelatine
130g finely grated unpeeled apple
500g greek-style yogurt
1 tablespoon passionfruit pulp

1 Stir honey and juice in small saucepan over low heat until honey melts; cool syrup 5 minutes.
2 Sprinkle gelatine over syrup; stir until gelatine dissolves.
3 Combine gelatine mixture, apple and yogurt. Pour into medium heatproof bowl and refrigerate until chilled. Pour yogurt mixture into ice-cream maker and churn according to manufacturer's instructions. (Or pour into 14cm x 21cm loaf tin, cover with foil and freeze 3 hours or overnight. Remove from freezer 15 minutes before serving.)
4 Divide yogurt among serving glasses; top each with 1 teaspoon of pulp.

prep + cook time 20 minutes + chilling, churning & freezing time
serves 4
tip You will need one green apple weighing about 275g for this recipe.

PASSIONFRUIT FROZEN YOGURT

110g caster sugar
60ml water
1 teaspoon gelatine
560g low-fat yogurt
125ml passionfruit pulp

1 Combine sugar and the water in small saucepan, stirring over low heat until sugar dissolves; transfer to medium jug.
2 Sprinkle gelatine over sugar syrup, stirring until gelatine dissolves.
3 Combine yogurt and pulp in jug with syrup; refrigerate until chilled. Pour yogurt mixture into ice-cream maker and churn according to manufacturer's instructions. (Or pour yogurt mixture into loaf tin, cover tightly with foil; freeze 3 hours or until almost set. Scrape yogurt from bottom and sides of tin with fork; return to freezer until firm.)

prep + cook time 15 minutes + chilling, churning & freezing time
serves 4
tip You will need 6 medium passionfruit for this recipe.

MANGO VANILLA FROZEN YOGURT SWIRLS

330ml mango purée
55g icing sugar
375g greek-style yogurt
1 teaspoon vanilla paste
(or vanilla extract)

1 Combine purée, 1 tablespoon of the sifted icing sugar and 2 tablespoons of the yogurt in small bowl.
2 Combine remaining sifted icing sugar, yogurt and vanilla paste in another small bowl.
3 Spoon a third of the mango mixture into eight 80ml ice-lolly moulds. Top with half the yogurt mixture; swirl with a skewer. Repeat with remaining mango and yogurt mixtures.
4 Press lids firmly on ice-lolly moulds, insert ice-lolly sticks if desired. Freeze 6 hours or overnight.

prep time 25 minutes + freezing time
serves 8
tip You will need two medium mangoes (860g) for this recipe.

SORBETS, GRANITAS & ICE-LOLLIES

TRIO OF ASIAN-FLAVOUR SORBETS

LEMONGRASS

2 x 10cm sticks fresh lemongrass (40g), chopped finely
220g caster sugar
625ml water
180ml lemon juice
yellow food colouring
1 egg white

1 Stir lemongrass, sugar and the water in medium saucepan over high heat until sugar dissolves; bring to a boil. Reduce heat; simmer, uncovered, without stirring, 5 minutes. Transfer to large heatproof jug, refrigerate until chilled.
2 Stir in juice and tint with food colouring. Pour into ice-cream maker and churn according to manufacturer's instructions, adding egg white during last 2–3 minutes of churning. (Or pour mixture into 14cm x 21cm loaf tin, cover tightly with foil; freeze 3 hours or overnight. Process mixture with egg white until smooth. Return to tin, cover; freeze until firm.)

prep + cook time 30 minutes + chilling, churning & freezing time
serves 8

BLOOD ORANGE

3 teaspoons finely grated blood orange rind
220g caster sugar
625ml water
180ml blood orange juice
red food colouring
1 egg white

1 Stir rind, sugar and the water in medium saucepan over high heat until sugar dissolves; bring to a boil. Reduce heat; simmer, uncovered, without stirring, 5 minutes. Transfer to large heatproof jug, refrigerate until chilled.
2 Stir in juice and tint with food colouring. Pour into ice-cream maker and churn according to manufacturer's instructions, adding egg white during last 2–3 minutes of churning. (Or pour mixture into 14cm x 21cm loaf tin, cover tightly with foil; freeze 3 hours or overnight. Process mixture with egg white until smooth. Return to tin, cover; freeze until firm.)

prep + cook time 30 minutes + chilling, churning & freezing time
serves 8

KAFFIR LIME

3 fresh kaffir lime leaves, chopped finely
220g caster sugar
625ml water
180ml lime juice
green food colouring
1 egg white

1 Stir lime leaves, sugar and the water in medium saucepan over high heat until sugar dissolves; bring to a boil. Reduce heat; simmer, uncovered, without stirring, 5 minutes. Transfer to large heatproof jug, refrigerate until chilled.
2 Stir in juice and tint with food colouring. Pour into ice-cream maker and churn according to manufacturer's instructions, adding egg white during last 2–3 minutes of churning. (Or pour mixture into 14cm x 21cm loaf tin, cover tightly with foil; freeze 3 hours or overnight. Process mixture with egg white until smooth. Return to tin, cover; freeze until firm.)

prep + cook time 30 minutes + chilling, churning & freezing time
serves 8

MANGO SORBET

220g granulated sugar
250ml water
80ml lemon juice
4 medium mangoes (1.7kg), peeled, chopped coarsely
2 egg whites, beaten lightly

1 Combine sugar and the water in medium saucepan. Stir over medium heat, without boiling, until sugar dissolves; add juice. Bring to a boil; reduce heat. Simmer, uncovered, 5 minutes. Pour into medium heatproof jug; refrigerate until chilled.
2 Blend or process mango until smooth. Add lemon syrup and egg whites; process until combined.
3 Pour into ice-cream maker and churn according to manufacturer's instructions. (Or pour mixture into freezer-proof container. Cover; freeze until sorbet is just firm. Chop sorbet; process mixture until smooth. Return sorbet to container. Cover; freeze until firm.)

prep + cook time 30 minutes + chilling, churning & freezing time
serves 6
tips For best results use fresh mango. Mango sorbet can be made a week ahead.

TRIO OF FRUITY SORBETS

LEMON LIME

2 tablespoons finely grated lemon rind
1 tablespoon finely grated lime rind
220g caster sugar
625ml water
125ml lemon juice
60ml lime juice
1 egg white

1 Stir rinds, sugar and the water in medium saucepan over high heat until sugar dissolves; bring to the boil. Reduce heat; simmer without stirring, uncovered, 5 minutes. Transfer to large heatproof jug, refrigerate until chilled.
2 Stir in juices; pour into ice-cream maker and churn according to manufacturer's instructions, adding egg white during last 2–3 minutes of churning. (Or pour sorbet mixture into loaf tin, cover tightly with foil; freeze 3 hours or overnight. Process mixture with egg white until smooth. Return to loaf tin, cover; freeze until firm.)

prep + cook time 30 minutes + chilling, churning & freezing time
serves 8

PASSIONFRUIT

250ml passionfruit pulp
220g caster sugar
625ml water
60ml lemon juice
2 egg whites

1 Strain pulp into small bowl. Reserve seeds and juice.
2 Stir sugar and the water in medium saucepan over high heat until sugar dissolves; bring to the boil. Reduce heat; simmer without stirring, uncovered, 5 minutes. Transfer to large heatproof jug, refrigerate until chilled.
3 Stir in lemon and passionfruit juices; pour into ice-cream maker and churn according to manufacturer's instructions, adding egg whites and reserved seeds during last 2–3 minutes of churning. (Or pour sorbet mixture into loaf tin, cover tightly with foil; freeze 3 hours or overnight. Process mixture with egg whites until smooth; stir in reserved seeds. Return to loaf tin, cover; freeze until firm.)

prep + cook time 30 minutes + chilling, churning & freezing time
serves 8

RASPBERRY

360g raspberries
220g caster sugar
625ml water
1 tablespoon lemon juice
1 egg white

1 Press raspberries through sieve into small bowl; discard seeds.
2 Stir sugar and the water in medium saucepan over high heat until sugar dissolves; bring to the boil. Reduce heat; simmer without stirring, uncovered, 5 minutes. Transfer to large heatproof jug, refrigerate until chilled.
3 Stir in raspberry pulp and lemon juice; pour into ice-cream maker and churn according to manufacturer's instructions, adding egg white during last 2–3 minutes of churning. (Or pour sorbet mixture into loaf tin, cover tightly with foil; freeze 3 hours or overnight. Process mixture with egg white until smooth. Return to loaf tin, cover; freeze until firm.)

prep + cook time 30 minutes + chilling, churning & freezing time
serves 8

SOFT GRAPE ICE WITH NUTMEG WAFERS

1.5kg seedless white grapes, approximately
3 egg whites
165g caster sugar

nutmeg wafers
1 egg white
55g caster sugar
2 tablespoons plain flour
½ teaspoon ground nutmeg
30g butter, melted
2 teaspoons cocoa powder

1 Discard grape stalks; process grapes until smooth. Push mixture through coarse strainer, pressing firmly to extract as much juice as possible. You need 810ml juice. Pour juice into large shallow cake tin. Cover with foil; freeze until just firm.

2 Beat egg whites in small bowl with electric mixer until soft peaks form. Gradually add sugar; beat until dissolved between additions.

3 Transfer frozen juice to large bowl; quickly beat with electric mixer until just smooth. Add egg white mixture; beat until combined and smooth.

4 Return mixture to tin. Cover; freeze until firm.

5 Serve grape ice with nutmeg wafers.

nutmeg wafers Preheat oven to 180°C/160°C fan-assisted. Beat egg white in small bowl with electric mixer until soft peaks form. Gradually add sugar; beat until dissolved between additions. Stir in flour and nutmeg, then cooled butter; reserve 2 tablespoons of the egg mixture. Place teaspoons of egg mixture about 10cm apart on baking parchment-lined baking trays, allowing four per tray; spread with spatula to about 7cm rounds. Combine reserved mixture with cocoa in small bowl; mix well. Spoon mixture into piping bag fitted with small plain tube. Pipe circles onto wafers to represent grapes. Bake, uncovered, about 5 minutes or until wafers are browned lightly. Lift wafers carefully from trays; place over handle of wooden spoon to give irregularly round shapes. Cool on wire racks.

prep + cook time about 1 hour + freezing time
serves 8
tips The high sugar content of this dessert will ensure the dessert remains soft and will not freeze solid. Grape ice can be made 3 days in advance.

PINEAPPLE ICE

1 large pineapple (2kg), chopped coarsely
165g caster sugar
500ml water
3 tablespoons finely chopped fresh mint leaves
4 egg whites

1 Blend or process pineapple until puréed; push through sieve into medium bowl. Discard pulp.
2 Combine sugar and the water in medium saucepan; stir over low heat until sugar dissolves. Bring to a boil; reduce heat. Simmer, uncovered, without stirring, about 10 minutes or until syrup thickens slightly. Cool then stir in mint.
3 Stir syrup into pineapple juice. Pour into medium heatproof jug; refrigerate until chilled if using ice-cream maker. Pour into ice-cream maker and churn according to manufacturer's instructions, adding egg whites during last 2–3 minutes of churning. (Or stir syrup into pineapple juice, cover with foil; freeze about 3 hours or until just set. Remove mixture from freezer; using fork, scrape mixture to break up then place in large bowl with egg whites. Beat with electric mixer until smooth. Pour mixture into 19cm x 29cm baking tin, cover with foil; freeze overnight. Stir occasionally while freezing to distribute mixture evenly.)
6 Serve pineapple ice with pieces of extra fresh pineapple, if you like.

prep + cook time 30 minutes + chilling, churning & freezing time
serves 4

PINK GRAPEFRUIT ICE WITH HAZELNUT WAFERS

250ml water
220g granulated sugar
250ml fresh pink grapefruit juice
60ml lemon juice
2 egg whites

hazelnut wafers
1 egg white
55g caster sugar
2 tablespoons ground hazelnuts
20g low-fat spread, melted

1 Stir the water and sugar in small saucepan over heat, without boiling, until sugar dissolves. Bring to a boil; boil 5 minutes without stirring. Remove from heat; stir in juices, cool.
2 Using electric mixer, beat egg whites in small bowl until soft peaks form. Fold grapefruit syrup into egg white mixture; pour into 10cm x 24cm loaf tin. Cover; freeze 3 hours or overnight.
3 Blend or process mixture until pale and creamy. Return to loaf tin, cover; freeze 3 hours or overnight. Serve grapefruit ice with hazelnut wafers.

hazelnut wafers Preheat oven to 180°C/160°C fan-assisted. Grease two oven trays; line each with baking parchment. Using electric mixer, beat egg white in small bowl until soft peaks form; gradually add sugar, beating until sugar dissolves between additions. Add ground hazelnuts and spread; stir until combined. Trace 16 x 7cm circles, 2cm apart, on lined trays. Spread a teaspoon of mixture in each circle. Bake for about 5 minutes or until lightly browned. Cool wafers on trays before carefully peeling away parchment.

prep + cook time 30 minutes + freezing time
serves 8
tip You will need two large pink grapefruit for this recipe.

WATERMELON & MINT GRANITA

500ml water
220g granulated sugar
1.6kg coarsely chopped watermelon
3 handfuls fresh mint leaves

1 Combine the water and sugar in medium saucepan. Stir over low heat, without boiling, until sugar dissolves; bring to the boil. Reduce heat; simmer, uncovered, without stirring, about 5 minutes or until syrup thickens slightly but does not colour.
2 Blend or process watermelon and mint, in batches, until almost smooth; push batches through sieve into large bowl. Add syrup; stir to combine.
3 Pour into medium heatproof jug, refrigerate until chilled. Pour into ice-cream maker and churn according to manufacturer's instructions until slushy but not completely frozen. Pour into two 20cm x 30cm baking tins. Cover with foil; freeze until firm. Scrape granita from bottom and sides of tin with a fork. Cover, return to freezer and repeat until large ice crystals form and granita has dry, shard-like appearance. Scrape again with fork before serving. (Or pour mixture into two 20cm x 30cm baking tins, cover with foil; freeze about 3 hours or until almost set. Using fork, scrape granita from bottom and sides of pans, mixing frozen with unfrozen mixture. Cover, return to freezer. Repeat process every hour for about 4 hours or until large ice crystals form and granita has a dry, shard-like appearance. Scrape again with fork before serving.)

prep + cook time 20 minutes + chilling, churning & freezing time
serves 8
tip You need half a large seedless watermelon (about 3kg) to get the amount of chopped watermelon needed for this recipe.

MUSCAT GRANITA WITH FRESH FIGS IN HONEY & FENNEL SYRUP

250ml water
125ml muscat
110g caster sugar
1 teaspoon black peppercorns
1 teaspoon finely grated lemon rind
1 tablespoon lemon juice
8 large fresh figs (640g)

honey & fennel syrup
1 tablespoon fennel seeds
125ml water
90g honey

1 Combine the water, muscat, sugar, peppercorns, rind and juice in small saucepan; bring to a boil.
2 Cool 10 minutes and strain into medium heatproof jug, refrigerate until chilled. Pour into ice-cream maker and churn according to manufacturer's instructions until slushy but not completely frozen. Pour into 14cm x 21cm loaf tin. Cover with foil; freeze until firm. Scrape granita from bottom and sides of tin with a fork. Cover, return to freezer and repeat until large ice crystals form and granita has dry, shard-like appearance. (Or cool mixture 10 minutes and strain into 14cm x 21cm loaf tin. Cover with foil; freeze about 4 hours or until firm. Scrape granita from bottom and sides of tin with a fork. Cover, return to freezer and repeat until large ice crystals form and granita has dry, shard-like appearance.)
3 Make honey & fennel syrup.
4 Cut figs lengthways into five slices; divide among serving plates, drizzle with syrup, top with granita.

honey & fennel syrup Dry-fry fennel seeds in small saucepan until fragrant. Add the water and honey; bring to a boil. Reduce heat; simmer, uncovered, without stirring, about 5 minutes or until mixture thickens slightly. Strain through sieve into small jug; discard seeds. Cool syrup 10 minutes before using.

prep + cook time 25 minutes + chilling, churning & freezing time
serves 4
tips Tokay, sweet riesling or gewürztraminer can be substituted for the muscat in the granita; drink what remains of the wine with this dessert.

PINEAPPLE & MINT ICE-LOLLIES

375ml pineapple juice
2 tablespoons icing sugar
2 teaspoons finely chopped fresh mint

1 Combine ingredients in medium jug. Pour mixture into six 60ml ice-lolly moulds; insert ice-lolly stick in the centre of each mould. Press lids on firmly; freeze 6 hours or overnight.

prep + cook time 5 minutes + freezing time
serves 6
tip To remove ice-lollies from moulds, dip into hot water for a few seconds, loosen lids and squeeze sides of moulds – the ice-lollies should slide out easily.

RASPBERRY ICE-LOLLIES

150g frozen raspberries
55g icing sugar
250ml sparkling mineral water

1 Heat raspberries and icing sugar in small saucepan over low heat, stirring occasionally, about 5 minutes or until raspberries soften. Using back of large spoon, push raspberry mixture through sieve into medium heatproof jug; discard seeds.

2 Stir mineral water into jug. Pour mixture into six 60ml ice-lolly moulds; insert ice-lolly stick in the centre of each mould. Press lids on firmly; freeze 6 hours or overnight.

prep + cook time 15 minutes + freezing time
serves 6

STRAWBERRY & PEACH TEQUILA ICE-LOLLIES

3 medium peaches
4 tablespoons grated palm sugar
80ml tequila
20ml Cointreau
20ml lemon juice
500g strawberries, coarsely chopped

1 Blend or process peaches until smooth.
2 Push peaches through a sieve into a medium bowl; stir in 2 tablespoons of the palm sugar, 40ml of the tequila, the Cointreau and lemon juice. Divide half the peach mixture into 12 x 80ml lolly moulds; reserve remaining peach mixture. Freeze lollies about 30 minutes or until surface is firm.
3 Meanwhile, blend or process strawberries until smooth. Push strawberries through a sieve into a medium bowl; stir in the remaining palm sugar and tequila. Press lolly stick firmly into each lolly. Divide half the strawberry mixture into moulds; reserve remaining strawberry mixture. Freeze lollies about 30 minutes or until surface is firm.
4 Divide remaining peach mixture into moulds; freeze lollies about 30 minutes or until surface is firm. Divide remaining strawberry mixture into moulds; freeze overnight.

prep time 30 minutes + freezing time
makes 12

FOUR LUSCIOUS LOLLIES

WATERMELON & STRAWBERRY

80ml water
2 tablespoons caster sugar
250g piece watermelon, peeled, deseeded, chopped coarsely
80g strawberries, chopped coarsely
2 teaspoons lemon juice

1 Combine the water and sugar in small saucepan; stir over low heat until sugar dissolves. Bring to the boil; boil, uncovered about 2 minutes or until mixture thickens slightly. Transfer syrup to small bowl; refrigerate until cold.
2 Blend or process cold syrup, watermelon, strawberries and juice until smooth. Pour mixture into four 80ml ice-lolly moulds; insert ice-lolly stick in the centre of each mould.
3 Freeze overnight until firm.

prep + cook time 15 minutes + chilling & freezing time
serves 4

HONEY, BANANA & YOGURT

1 large banana (230g)
190g vanilla yogurt
1 tablespoon honey

1 Blend or process ingredients until mixture is smooth and creamy. Pour into four 80ml ice-lolly moulds; insert ice-lolly stick in the centre of each mould.
2 Freeze overnight until firm.

prep time 5 minutes + freezing time
serves 4

LEMONADE, LEMON & MINT

375ml lemonade
1 teaspoon finely grated lemon rind
1 tablespoon lemon juice
2 teaspoons finely chopped mint

1 Combine ingredients in medium freezerproof jug; freeze mixture about 1 hour until partially frozen. Stir; pour mixture into four 80ml ice-lolly moulds; insert ice-lolly stick in the centre of each mould.
2 Freeze overnight until firm.

prep time 5 minutes + freezing time
serves 4

SPICED COFFEE

2 teaspoons instant coffee
2 teaspoons drinking chocolate
2 teaspoons caster sugar
¼ teaspoon ground cinnamon
1 tablespoon boiling water
160ml double cream, whipped lightly

1 Combine coffee, drinking chocolate, sugar and cinnamon in medium jug. Add the water, stirring until sugar dissolves, cool 5 minutes; gently stir in cream. Pour mixture into four 80ml ice-lolly moulds; insert ice-lolly stick in the centre of each mould.
2 Freeze overnight until firm.

prep time 5 minutes + cooling and freezing time
serves 4

AFTER DINNER MINT ICES

2 eggs, separated
1 tablespoon caster sugar
50g dark eating chocolate, melted
2 tablespoons mint-flavoured liqueur
160ml double cream

1 Beat egg yolks and sugar in small bowl with electric mixer until thick and creamy; beat in chocolate and liqueur. Transfer to medium bowl.
2 Beat cream in small bowl with electric mixer until soft peaks form; fold into chocolate mixture.
3 Beat egg whites in small bowl with electric mixer until soft peaks form; fold into chocolate mixture.
4 Pour mixture into eight 60ml ice-lolly moulds; push lolly sticks into centre of each mould. Press lids on firmly; freeze overnight.

prep time 20 minutes + freezing time
serves 8

FROZEN DESSERTS

BANANA SPLIT

- 4 medium bananas (800g), halved lengthways
- 2 tablespoons brown sugar
- 100g dark eating chocolate
- 300ml double cream
- 1 tablespoon dark rum
- 4 scoops (240ml) vanilla ice-cream (see page 12)
- 4 scoops (240ml) chocolate ice-cream (see page 12)
- 80g coarsely chopped roasted pecans
- 25g toasted shredded coconut

1 Preheat grill.

2 Place bananas, cut-sides up, on oven tray; sprinkle with sugar. Grill about 3 minutes or until sugar melts.

3 Meanwhile, melt chocolate with 2 tablespoons of the cream in small bowl set over small saucepan of simmering water (do not let water touch base of bowl).

4 Beat remaining cream with rum in small bowl with electric mixer until soft peaks form.

5 Place 2 banana halves in each of four dishes; top each with a scoop of the vanilla and chocolate ice-cream then drizzle with chocolate. Top with cream and sprinkle with nuts and coconut. Serve immediately

prep + cook time 30 minutes
serves 4

LEMON BOMBES ALASKA

680ml vanilla ice-cream (see page 12), softened slightly
30g unsalted butter
½ teaspoon finely grated lemon rind
1 tablespoon lemon juice
1 egg yolk
55g caster sugar
80ml limoncello
125ml double cream
290g bought sponge cake
2 egg whites
75g caster sugar, extra

1 Line four 125ml moulds with cling film. Press about 80ml ice-cream firmly up and around inside of each mould to form cavity. Cover with foil; freeze 2 hours. Return remaining ice-cream to freezer.
2 Combine butter, rind, juice, yolk and sugar in small heatproof bowl; stir over small saucepan of simmering water until mixture thickens slightly. Stir in liqueur. Cover surface of lemon curd with cling film; refrigerate until cold.
3 Place 1 tablespoon of the lemon curd into each mould, cover; freeze until firm. Combine remaining lemon curd with cream, cover; refrigerate lemon cream until serving.
4 Remove moulds from the freezer, spread enough remaining ice-cream over lemon curd to fill moulds; cover, freeze bombes until firm.
5 Preheat oven to 240°C/220°C fan-assisted.
6 Cut four rounds from sponge cake, large enough to cover top of each mould.
7 Beat egg whites in small bowl with electric mixer until soft peaks form; add extra sugar, 1 tablespoon at a time, beating until sugar dissolves between additions.
8 Turn one bombe onto one round of sponge cake on oven tray; peel away cling film. Spread a quarter of the meringue mixture over to enclose bombe completely; repeat to make a total of four bombes.
9 Bake bombes, uncovered, about 3 minutes or until browned lightly. Serve immediately with lemon cream.

prep + cook time 1 hour + chilling & freezing time
serves 4
tip Bombes can be prepared the day before serving to the stage at which they are ready to be baked; freeze until ready to bake.

PEANUT BUTTER & FUDGE ICE-CREAM PIE

300g packet chocolate chip cookies
40g butter, melted
1 tablespoon milk
1 litre vanilla ice-cream (see page 12), softened slightly
375g crunchy peanut butter

hot marshmallow fudge sauce
200g dark eating chocolate, chopped coarsely
50g white marshmallows, chopped coarsely
300ml double cream

1 Grease 24cm-round loose-based flan tin.
2 Blend or process cookies until mixture resembles coarse breadcrumbs. Add butter and milk; process until combined.
3 Press cookie mixture evenly over base and around side of prepared tin; refrigerate 10 minutes.
4 Beat softened ice-cream and peanut butter in large bowl with electric mixer until combined. Spoon filling into crumb crust. Cover; freeze pie for 3 hours or overnight.
5 Make hot marshmallow fudge sauce.
6 Drizzle slices of pie with hot sauce to serve.

hot marshmallow fudge sauce
Combine ingredients in small saucepan; stir over heat, without boiling, until smooth.

prep + cook time 30 minutes + chilling & freezing time
serves 10
tip Warm a large knife under hot water, quickly dry it and cut the pie while the knife is still hot.

BROWNIE ICE-CREAM STACKS WITH HOT MOCHA FUDGE SAUCE

500ml vanilla ice-cream (see page 12), softened slightly
80g butter
150g dark eating chocolate, chopped coarsely
150g brown sugar
2 eggs, beaten lightly
75g plain flour
60g soured cream
50g walnuts, chopped coarsely

hot mocha fudge sauce
50g dark eating chocolate, chopped coarsely
125ml double cream
2 tablespoons brown sugar
½ teaspoon instant coffee granules
1 tablespoon coffee-flavoured liqueur

1 Line base and sides of 8cm x 26cm shallow cake tin with baking parchment. Press ice-cream into tin, cover with foil; freeze overnight.
2 Preheat oven to 180C/160°C fan-assisted. Line base and sides of another 8cm x 26cm shallow cake tin with baking parchment.
3 Combine butter and chocolate in small saucepan; stir over low heat until mixture is smooth. Transfer chocolate mixture to medium bowl. Stir in sugar; cool.
4 Stir eggs then sifted flour, soured cream and nuts into chocolate mixture. Spread mixture into prepared tin; bake, uncovered, in oven about 40 minutes. Cool brownie in tin.
5 Meanwhile, make hot mocha fudge sauce.
6 Turn brownie onto wire rack; remove paper. Trim narrow ends; cut brownie into 12 slices.
7 Turn ice-cream out of tin; cut into eight slices. Stack alternate slices of ice-cream and brownie starting and finishing with brownie. Drizzle each stack with hot mocha fudge sauce.

hot mocha fudge sauce Combine chocolate, cream, sugar and coffee in small saucepan. Stir over low heat until mixture is smooth; bring to the boil. Reduce heat; simmer, uncovered, 2 minutes. Remove from heat; stir in liqueur.

prep + cook time about 1 hour + cooling & freezing time
serves 4

CHOCOLATE, NUT & COFFEE ICE-CREAM CAKE

- 2 litres vanilla ice-cream (see page 12)
- 1 tablespoon instant coffee granules
- 1 tablespoon hot water
- 70g caramelised almonds, chopped coarsely
- 100g dark eating chocolate, melted
- 1 tablespoon crème de cacao
- 100g white eating chocolate, melted
- 75g roasted pistachios, chopped coarsely

1 Grease 21cm springform tin; line base and side with baking parchment.

2 Divide ice-cream into three portions; return two portions to freezer. Soften remaining ice-cream in medium bowl.

3 Dissolve coffee in the water in small jug, cool; stir into softened ice-cream with two-thirds of the almonds. Spoon into prepared tin, cover; freeze about 2 hours or until firm.

4 Soften second portion of ice-cream in medium bowl; stir in dark eating chocolate. Microwave, uncovered, on MEDIUM-HIGH (80%) about 2 minutes or until chocolate melts; whisk until smooth. Stir in liqueur, cover; freeze about 1 hour or until almost firm. Spoon dark chocolate ice-cream over coffee layer, cover; freeze about 2 hours or until firm.

5 Soften remaining ice-cream in medium bowl; fold in white chocolate. Microwave, uncovered, on MEDIUM-HIGH (80%) about 2 minutes or until chocolate melts; whisk until smooth. Stir in two-thirds of the pistachios, cover; freeze about 1 hour or until almost firm, stirring ice-cream occasionally to suspend pistachios evenly. Spoon white chocolate ice-cream over dark chocolate layer, cover; freeze about 2 hours or until firm.

6 Remove ice-cream cake from tin just before serving; sprinkle with remaining nuts.

prep time 35 minutes + cooling & freezing time
serves 10
tips It is important each layer sets firm before adding the next. To remove ice-cream cake easily, rub sides of tin with a hot cloth. If caramelised almonds are not available, you can use chopped toasted almonds instead.

BANANA CARAMEL SUNDAE

70g dark eating chocolate, chopped finely
70g roasted walnuts, chopped coarsely
1 litre vanilla ice-cream (see page 12)
4 medium bananas (800g), chopped coarsely

caramel sauce
100g butter
125ml double cream
110g brown sugar

1 Make caramel sauce.
2 Divide one-third of the sauce among six 180ml glasses; divide half the chocolate, nuts, ice-cream and banana among glasses. Repeat layering process, ending with a layer of the sauce.

caramel sauce Combine ingredients in small saucepan. Stir over low heat until sugar dissolves; bring to the boil. Reduce heat; simmer, uncovered, 5 minutes. Cool.

prep + cook time 20 minutes
serves 6

GLACÉ FRUIT & CITRUS FROZEN PUDDINGS WITH BITTER ORANGE SAUCE

280g finely chopped mixed glacé fruit
170g orange marmalade
2 tablespoons orange juice
2 teaspoons finely grated orange rind
3 tablespoons coarsely chopped fresh mint
2 litres vanilla ice-cream (see page 12), softened slightly

bitter orange sauce
160ml orange juice
115g orange marmalade
2 tablespoons lemon juice

1 Line eight individual 250ml moulds with cling film.
2 Combine fruit, marmalade, juice, rind and mint in medium bowl.
3 Place ice-cream in large bowl; fold in fruit mixture. Divide mixture among prepared moulds; cover with foil. Freeze puddings 3 hours or overnight.
4 Make bitter orange sauce.
5 Turn puddings out of moulds onto serving plates; serve with bitter orange sauce.

bitter orange sauce Combine ingredients in small jug

prep time 20 minutes
serves 8

NAGANO UNIQLO NAGANOMINAMI BYPASS 4-21-25 INAZATOMACHI NAGANO-SHI
UNIQLO KAKAMIGAHARAMITSUIKE 2-195-5 UNUMAMITSUIKE
OHKIDPARK NISHI2F 2-23 KOURAN GIFU-SHI GIFU UNIQLO GIFU
306-2 SAGIYAMA SENDO GIFU-SHI GIFU UNIQLO HIDATAKAYAMA

CHOCOMARMALASKA

4 large chocolate muffins (460g)
115g orange marmalade
250ml chocolate ice-cream (see page 12)
3 egg whites
165g brown sugar
1 teaspoon finely grated orange rind

1 Cut tops off muffins; discard. Hollow out muffin centres, leaving a 1cm border.
2 Drop level tablespoons of marmalade into each muffin. Top with ice-cream. Stand muffins on oven tray, freeze about 1 hour or until firm.
3 Preheat oven to 240°C/220°C fan-assisted.
4 Just before serving, beat egg whites in small bowl with electric mixer until soft peaks form; gradually add sugar, beating until dissolved between additions. Beat in orange rind.
5 Spread meringue over muffins. Bake about 2 minutes or until browned lightly. Serve immediately.

prep + cook time 20 minutes + freezing time
serves 4

COCO-CHERRY ICE-CREAM TIMBALES

2 litres vanilla ice-cream (see page 12)
3 x 50g dark chocolate Bounty bars, chopped coarsely
140g toasted almonds, chopped coarsely
50g glacé cherries, chopped coarsely
50g pink marshmallows, chopped coarsely
50g dark chocolate, chopped coarsely
pink food colouring

white chocolate sauce
300ml double cream
100g white chocolate, chopped finely

1 Soften ice-cream in large bowl; stir in chopped Bounty bars, almonds, cherries, marshmallows, dark chocolate and enough colouring to tint the ice-cream pink. Divide mixture among eight 250ml moulds. Cover with foil; freeze 3 hours or overnight.
2 Make white chocolate sauce.
3 Turn ice-cream timbales onto serving plates; drizzle with warm white chocolate sauce.

white chocolate sauce Place cream in small saucepan; bring to a boil. Remove from heat; add white chocolate. Stir until chocolate melts.

prep + cook time 12 minutes + freezing time
serves 8

ACCOMPANIMENTS

CHOCOLATE FUDGE SAUCE

200g dark eating chocolate
20g unsalted butter
¼ teaspoon vanilla extract
125ml double cream

1 Place chocolate and butter in small heatproof bowl set over small saucepan of simmering water; do not allow water to touch base of bowl. Stir until chocolate is melted. Add extract and cream; stir until combined. Serve sauce warm.

prep + cook time 15 minutes
makes 250ml
tip Sauce will keep under refrigeration, covered, for up to three days. To serve, reheat sauce briefly in microwave oven on HIGH (100%) or over low heat in small saucepan until it reaches the desired consistency.

FOUR INDULGENT SAUCES

MARS BAR & MARSHMALLOW

4 x 60g Mars bars, chopped finely
300ml double cream
100g packet marshmallows

1 Stir Mars bars and cream in small saucepan, over low heat, until smooth. Add marshmallows, stir until smooth.

prep + cook time 20 minutes
makes 500ml
tips Replace Mars bars with other chocolate such as Snickers or Bounty bars. Liqueur can be added to create a different flavour, if desired. Make sure heat is low, if the heat is too high, the chocolate will form firm balls and won't melt.

BUTTERSCOTCH

220g caster sugar
125ml water
300ml double cream

1 Combine sugar and the water in small saucepan; stir over low heat until sugar dissolves. Boil, uncovered, without stirring, about 15 minutes or until mixture turns a caramel colour.
2 Remove from heat; allow bubbles to subside. Gradually add cream, stirring constantly, over low heat, until sauce is smooth. Cool 10 minutes.

prep + cook time 25 minutes
makes 375ml

WHITE CHOC, ORANGE & COCONUT

160ml double cream
10cm strip orange rind
2 cardamom pods, bruised
180g white eating chocolate, chopped coarsely
2 teaspoons coconut-flavoured liqueur

1 Place cream, orange rind and cardamom pods in small saucepan; bring to a boil. Remove from heat.
2 Add chocolate and liqueur; stir until smooth. Strain sauce; discard cardamom pods and rind.

prep + cook time 15 minutes
makes 250ml

STRAWBERRY COULIS

300g frozen strawberries, thawed
1 tablespoon icing sugar

1 Push berries through fine sieve into small bowl; discard seeds. Stir sifted icing sugar into sauce.

prep time 10 minutes
makes 250ml
tips Any berries, fresh or frozen, can be used; blend or process berries until smooth, then continue as above. Other fruits such as mango, passionfruit, kiwifruit, and even pineapple, can be used. Sugar should be adjusted according to the fruit used.

COFFEE LIQUEUR SAUCE

- 60ml double cream
- 160ml freshly brewed strong coffee
- 250g white eating chocolate, chopped coarsely
- 1 tablespoon coffee-flavoured liqueur

1 Combine cream and coffee in small saucepan; stir over medium heat, without boiling, until hot. Remove from heat; add chocolate, whisk until smooth. Stir in liqueur.
2 Transfer sauce to small bowl; cover, refrigerate about 30 minutes, stirring occasionally.

prep + cook time 20 minutes + chilling time
makes 500ml

FOUR CRUNCHY TOPPINGS

CHOCOLATE FRUIT & NUT BARK

1 tablespoon aniseed
200g dark eating chocolate, melted
120g finely chopped dried pears
65g finely chopped roasted macadamias

1 Dry-fry aniseed in small frying pan until fragrant; chop finely.
2 Warm a baking tray in oven; cover with baking parchment.
3 Combine aniseed with rest of ingredients in medium bowl.
4 Spread mixture onto tray as thinly as possible. Refrigerate until set then break into rough pieces.

prep + cook time 20 minutes + chilling time

CHOC-ALMOND CRUNCH

440g caster sugar
250ml water
200g dark eating chocolate, chopped coarsely
40g flaked almonds, roasted

1 Combine sugar and the water in medium heavy-based saucepan; stir over low heat until sugar dissolves. Increase heat; bring to the boil. Boil, uncovered, without stirring, about 10 minutes or until syrup is a deep golden colour.
2 Pour mixture into 20cm x 30cm baking tin; stand 5 minutes. Sprinkle chocolate over hot toffee, spreading with palette knife to completely cover. Sprinkle with nuts; refrigerate until set. Break into shards before serving.

prep + cook time 20 minutes + standing & chilling time

DARK CHOCOLATE PISTACHIO BRITTLE

440g caster sugar
125ml water
140g roasted pistachios, chopped coarsely
200g dark eating chocolate, melted

1 Line baking tray with baking parchment.
2 Combine sugar and the water in medium saucepan; stir over heat, without boiling, until sugar dissolves. Bring to the boil; boil, uncovered, without stirring, until golden brown. Allow bubbles to subside; add nuts. Pour mixture onto tray; leave to set at room temperature.
3 Spread chocolate over brittle; refrigerate about 10 minutes until chocolate sets. Break into pieces.

prep + cook time 20 minutes + standing & chilling time

POM POMS

395g sweetened condensed milk
30g unsalted butter
140g finely chopped roasted unsalted peanuts
40g air-popped popcorn
40g toasted shredded coconut
200g milk eating chocolate, melted

1 Line two baking trays with baking parchment.
2 Combine condensed milk and butter in large heavy-based saucepan; cook, stirring, over medium heat, about 10 minutes or until mixture is a caramel colour. Remove from heat; quickly stir in nuts, popcorn and coconut.
3 Working quickly, roll mixture into walnut-sized balls; dip in chocolate. Chill on trays until firm.

prep + cook time 20 minutes + chilling time

APPLE, CRANBERRY & WHITE CHOCOLATE BISCOTTI

220g caster sugar
2 eggs
200g plain flour
50g self-raising flour
35g finely chopped dried apple
65g coarsely chopped dried cranberries
90g white eating chocolate, grated coarsely

1 Preheat oven to 180°C/160°C fan-assisted. Grease baking tray.
2 Whisk sugar and eggs in medium bowl until combined; stir in sifted flours then apple, cranberries and chocolate.
3 Knead dough on floured surface until smooth. Divide dough in half, roll each portion into a 30cm log; place logs on tray. Bake about 30 minutes. Cool on tray 10 minutes.
4 Reduce oven temperature to 150°C/130°C fan-assisted.
5 Using serrated knife, cut logs diagonally into 5mm slices. Place slices, in single layer, on ungreased baking trays. Bake biscotti about 30 minutes or until dry and crisp, turning halfway through baking. Cool on wire racks.

prep + cook time 1 hour 25 minutes
makes 60
tip Biscotti will keep in an airtight container for at least a month.

CHOCOLATE HAZELNUT THINS

1 egg white
55g brown sugar
2 tablespoons plain flour
2 teaspoons cocoa powder
30g butter, melted
1 teaspoon milk
1 tablespoon ground hazelnuts

1 Preheat oven to 180°C/160°C fan-assisted. Grease baking trays.
2 Beat egg white in small bowl with electric mixer until soft peaks form; gradually add sugar, beating until sugar dissolves. Stir in sifted flour and cocoa, then butter, milk and ground hazelnuts.
3 Spread level teaspoons of mixture into 8cm circles, about 4cm apart on trays.
4 Bake thins, in batches, about 5 minutes. Remove from tray immediately using metal spatula, place over rolling pin to cool.

prep + cook time 25 minutes
makes 24

COCONUT SESAME CRISPS

1 teaspoon honey
20g butter
1 egg white
2 tablespoons caster sugar
2 tablespoons plain flour
1 tablespoon desiccated coconut
2 teaspoons sesame seeds

1 Stir honey and butter in small saucepan over low heat until smooth; cool.

2 Preheat oven to 160°C/140°C fan-assisted. Line two baking trays with baking parchment; mark four 7.5cm circles on paper on each tray, turn paper over.

3 Beat egg white in small bowl with electric mixer until soft peaks form; gradually add sugar, beating until dissolved. Fold in sifted flour and butter mixture.

4 Spread level teaspoons of mixture to fill centre of each circle on trays; sprinkle with combined coconut and seeds.

5 Bake one tray of crisps at a time for about 5 minutes. Remove crisps from tray immediately using metal spatula; place crisps over rolling pin to cool.

prep + cook time 1 hour
makes 28
tips You may find it easier to bake just two crisps on a tray at a time. Re-use the baking-parchment lining. Store crisps in an airtight container for up to a week.

MINI FLORENTINES

120g sultanas
80g corn flakes
60g roasted flaked almonds
100g red glacé cherries, quartered
160ml sweetened condensed milk
60g white eating chocolate, melted
60g dark eating chocolate, melted

1 Preheat oven to 180°C/160°C fan-assisted. Line oven trays with baking parchment.
2 Combine sultanas, corn flakes, nuts, cherries and condensed milk in medium bowl.
3 Drop tablespoons of mixture about 5cm apart on trays. Bake about 5 minutes; cool on trays.
4 Spread the bases of half the florentines with white chocolate; spread remaining florentine bases with dark chocolate. Run fork through chocolate to make waves; stand at room temperature until set.

prep + cook time 25 minutes + standing time
makes 25
tip Store florentines in an airtight container in the fridge for up to a week.

GLOSSARY

aniseed also called anise; the liquorice-flavoured seeds of the anise plant.
blood orange a virtually seedless citrus fruit with blood-red-streaked rind and flesh; sweet, non-acidic, salmon-coloured pulp and juice with slight strawberry or raspberry overtones. The rind is not as bitter as an ordinary orange.
buttermilk originally the term given to the slightly sour liquid left after butter was churned from cream, today it is commercially made similarly to yogurt. Sold alongside fresh milk products in supermarkets; low-fat yogurt or milk can be substituted. Despite the implication of its name, it is low in fat.
caramelised almonds almonds with a crisp toffee glaze.
cinnamon dried inner bark of the shoots of the cinnamon tree. Available as a stick or ground.
coconut
desiccated unsweetened and concentrated, dried finely shredded coconut flesh.
shredded thin strips of dried coconut flesh.
Cointreau orange-flavoured liqueur.
condensed milk a canned milk product consisting of milk with more than half the water content removed and sugar added to the milk that remains.
cranberries available fresh, frozen and dried; have a rich, astringent flavour and are used in sweet or savoury dishes. Dried cranberries have the same slightly sour, succulent flavour as fresh cranberries; can usually be substituted for or with other dried fruit in most recipes.
crème de cacao a liqueur made from cocoa beans and vanilla. It comes in two colours, dark and white (clear).
evaporated milk an unsweetened canned milk from which water has been extracted by evaporation.
fennel seeds dried seeds with a distinct liquorice flavour.
gelatine we used powdered gelatine; also available in sheet form known as leaf gelatine.
glacé fruit fruit such as cherries, peaches, pineapple, orange and citron cooked in heavy sugar syrup then dried. Available in specialty food stores, delicatessens and online.
green tea powder green tea leaves ground into a fine powder; sold, ready-ground, in small tins in Asian markets, specialty stores or online.
kaffir lime leaves aromatic leaves used fresh or dried in Asian dishes. Dried leaves are available in most good supermarkets; fresh leaves are available online, in Asian markets and specialty stores.
limoncello Italian lemon-flavoured liqueur. Made from the peel only of fragrant lemons, the peels are steeped in a good-quality clear alcohol then diluted with sugar and water.
muscat a sweet, aromatic dessert wine with an almost musty flavour. It is made with the fully matured muscatel grape.
nuts
almonds flat, pointy-ended nuts with pitted brown shell enclosing a creamy white kernel covered by brown skin.
hazelnuts also called filberts; plump, grape-sized, rich, sweet

nut with a brown skin (which can be removed by rubbing heated nuts together vigorously in a tea-towel). Ground hazelnuts are made by grinding hazelnuts to a coarse flour texture for use in baking or as a thickening agent. If you can't find ground, use roasted hazelnuts and grind in a food processor.

macadamias native to Australia, a rich and buttery nut; store in refrigerator because of its high oil content.

peanuts also known as ground nuts, these are not true nuts but a legume that grows underground in a pod.

pecans native to the United States; golden-brown, buttery and rich. Good in savoury and sweet dishes; especially good in salads.

pistachios pale green, delicately flavoured nut inside hard off-white shells. To peel, soak shelled nuts in boiling water about 5 minutes; drain, then pat dry.

nougat a traditional confectionery made from sugar and/or honey, roasted nuts and sometimes dried fruit and egg whites.

port a sweet, red, fortified wine produced in the Douro Valley of northern Portugal.

ricotta a soft, sweet, moist, white, cow's-milk cheese with a low fat content (about 8.5 per cent) and a slightly grainy texture. The name roughly translates as 'cooked again' and refers to ricotta's manufacture from a whey that is itself a by-product of other cheese making.

sesame seeds black and white are the most common of these tiny oval seeds; a good source of calcium.

sugar

granulated a coarse table sugar, also known as crystal sugar.

icing also known as confectioners' sugar, granulated suger ground to a soft, fine powder.

brown and light brown soft, fine granulated sugar retaining molasses for its characteristic colour and flavour.

caster also known as superfine or finely granulated table sugar.

sultanas also known as golden raisins; dried seedless white grapes.

tequila made from mixture of fresh and fermented agave juice (pulque); double-distilled to produce white (clear) tequila. Gold tequila is aged in oak casks for up to four years.

tofu also known as bean curd, an off-white, custard-like product made from the 'milk' of crushed soy beans; comes fresh as soft or firm, and processed as fried or pressed dried sheets. Leftover fresh tofu can be refrigerated in water (which is changed daily) up to four days. Silken tofu refers to the method by which it is made – where it is strained through silk.

vanilla

pod dried long, thin pod from a tropical golden orchid grown in central and South America and Tahiti; the minuscule black seeds inside the bean are used to impart a distinctively sweet vanilla flavour.

extract obtained from vanilla beans infused in water; a non-alcoholic version of essence.

paste a unique blend of concentrated pure vanilla extract and vanilla pods (including seeds) in an all-natural sugar syrup.

INDEX

CONVERSION CHARTS

measures

One metric tablespoon holds 20ml; one metric teaspoon holds 5ml.

All cup and spoon measurements are level. The most accurate way of measuring dry ingredients is to weigh them. When measuring liquids, use a clear glass or plastic jug with metric markings.

We use large eggs with an average weight of 60g.

dry measures

METRIC	IMPERIAL
15g	½oz
30g	1oz
60g	2oz
90g	3oz
125g	4oz (¼lb)
155g	5oz
185g	6oz
220g	7oz
250g	8oz (½lb)
280g	9oz
315g	10oz
345g	11oz
375g	12oz (¾lb)
410g	13oz
440g	14oz
470g	15oz
500g	16oz (1lb)
750g	24oz (1½lb)
1kg	32oz (2lb)

liquid measures

METRIC	IMPERIAL
30ml	1 fluid oz
60ml	2 fluid oz
100ml	3 fluid oz
125ml	4 fluid oz
150ml	5 fluid oz
190ml	6 fluid oz
250ml	8 fluid oz
300ml	10 fluid oz
500ml	16 fluid oz
600ml	20 fluid oz
1000ml (1 litre)	32 fluid oz

length measures

3mm	⅛in
6mm	¼in
1cm	½in
2cm	¾in
2.5cm	1in
5cm	2in
6cm	2½in
8cm	3in
10cm	4in
13cm	5in
15cm	6in
18cm	7in
20cm	8in
23cm	9in
25cm	10in
28cm	11in
30cm	12in (1ft)

oven temperatures

These are fan-assisted temperatures. If you have a conventional oven (ie. not fan-assisted), increase temperatures by 10–20°.

	°C (CELSIUS)	°F (FAHRENHEIT)	GAS MARK
Very low	100	210	½
Low	130	260	1–2
Moderately low	140	280	3
Moderate	160	325	4–5
Moderately hot	180	350	6
Hot	200	400	7–8
Very hot	220	425	9